Things

Stephen Wilson

BEN YEHUDA PRESS
Oxford
2013

By the same author:
Poems
Fluttering Hands (2008)

Fiction
Sonata in Four Movements (2012)

Criticism
The Cradle of Violence: Essays on Psychiatry, Psychoanalysis and Literature (1995)
Poetics of the Diaspora (2012)

Brief Biography
Sigmund Freud (1997, 2008) (Translated: Polish, 2001, Norwegian, 2002, Chinese 2002)
Isaac Rosenberg (2010)

Graphic Guide
Introducing the Freud Wars (2002, 2012)

Anthology
The Bloomsbury Book of the Mind (2003, 2004)

Ben Yehuda Press
Oxford

Things hard for thought

© Stephen Wilson 2013

First published in Great Britain in 2013
All rights reserved

This book is sold subject to the conditions that it shall not, by way of trade or otherwise, be lent, resold, hired out, or otherwise circulated without the copyright holder's prior consent in any form of binding or cover other than that in which it is published and without a similar condition including this condition being imposed on the subsequent purchaser.

ISBN-13: 978-148088401
ISBN-10: 148088409

For all my poet friends

Chinese Lear
As deep-fried Wan Tan
are we to the gods;
they dip us
in their sauce.

ACKNOWLEDGEMENTS

Some of these poems (or earlier versions) appeared in *The Hippocrates Prize Anthology, 2010, Magma, Oxford Magazine, Stand, Jewish Renaissance, Chest, The Rialto, The Flight of the Turtle:New Writing Scotland 29, Flarestack Poetry Anthology, 2012, The French Literary Review, The Liberal, Other Poetry, Star*Line, Poets Meet Politics, Hungry Hill, 2011, The Barnet Poetry Anthology, 2009, Bellevue Literary Revue, Poems in the Waiting Room, Out of the Ash, Aberystwyth Writing Project, 2006.*

I owe many thanks to Kate Wilson, Matthew Francis and Paula Jennings. 'Flood', 'Spoilage', 'Philosopher' and 'Lady Walk' were written in Hawthornden Castle. I am grateful for the Fellowship which allowed me to reside there throughout June 2010.

e Uranìe m'aiuti col suo coro
forti cose a pensar mettere in versi

Purgatorio, xxix

CONTENTS

Horse Sense	1
Cradle Song	3
Saying 'Good-Bye' to Grandchildren	4
Hibernaculum	5
Dr Maimonides (i)	6
Philosopher	8
Heritage	9
The Medieval Jewish Cemetery In Oxford	10
Buchenwald	11
Dr Maimonides (ii)	12
The Salon of Henriette Herz c. 1800	13
Musée Rodin	14
Spoilage	15
Koro	16
Flood	17
Trap Grounds	18
Lampyris noctiluca	19
Turdus merula	20
Perspective	21
Canzone	22
Aegithalos caudatus	23
Laundry Basket	24
Property of Tesco	25
Hirundo Rustica	26
Lady Walk	27
Frondeg / Winter in *Frondeg*	28
Alexandrian Duet	29
These forms	32
Lifting Anchor	33
Last Will	34
The Art of Disappearing	35

Horse Sense

Where we've stopped to watch,
the paddock gate's seasoned
with a sprinkling of hoar,
the ground's indurated with cold
and I'm holding you up to look,
remarking that today, even horses
are wearing their coats.
Your brow furrows for a moment,
before you ask how they put them on?
I can see the problem –
despite shoulder, elbow and knee
on the same limb, fetlock and pastern;
an abundance of joints which you'd think
made it possible to manoeuvre the aperture
in the cover over their heads; without hands
the praxis would obviously be difficult –
and we don't believe in magic.

I can only suggest that the horse
hoofs out the material on the field,
as if unrolling a carpet, and then
taking two corners (one by one) in its mouth,
carefully folds it along a central crease.
Bringing the front sides of the garment
into apposition, and leaving sufficient space
for its head to pass through, it nudges
the collar into existence, compressing
the top margins (that must be made
of velcro or have magnets sewn in the hem)
with a patting movement of its nose.
Then with an almighty kick,
it tosses the whole thing into the air,
exhaling hot gas through dilated nostrils
sufficient to produce a brief lift,
at the same time executing a capriole,
aiming itself as precisely as possible
at the neck-hole, like a footballer
leaping to head a goal. No doubt
several attempts are necessary,

and once having got the coat
on its back, some minor adjustments
brought about by extreme lateral flexion
of the cervical region, enable the collar
to be seized by the jaws and pulled forward.

We could imagine another method
that involves spreading the sheet out,
quickly doing a kind of Fosbury Flop
and somehow finishing legs up,
as if having a nappy changed;
then rubbing or shuffling along the ground
in such a way as to make the cloth
adhere to the dorsum, before springing off,
and in mid-air, clasping the neckpiece
together with the undersurface of the hooves
– but this seems implausible.

Cradle Song
for my granddaughter, Mia

Sleep, child, your arms raised in surrender,
sleep as a warm wind sleeps, as an oasis

in the sand. Sleep as a willow sleeps,
like a gliding bird. Sleep as a ship

sleeps on water, as the anchor sinks.
Sleep as indigo in the evening sea;

like a star cradled in the moon.
Sleep, child, like a white cloud;

sleep as a seed sleeps, as the billow
of lungs, as an unsung song.

Sleep as language sleeps, as history sleeps –
sleep today, as your mother slept in my arms.

Saying 'Good-bye' to Grandchildren

As we close the front door
an ice-age slithers in –
it's as if your whole species
had become extinct.
Nothing but morainic debris
and the tell-tale imprint
of cave-dwellers' hands
blown in umber through
the hollow of a bird bone.
And a plastic *glyptodon*
whose domed carapace
of overlapping scutes
we might have taken for shelter
ten thousand years ago, scaled
by the Natural History Museum
to the size of a hen's egg
balanced on four stubby legs,
abandoned on a plate
beside a bunch of bananas
and heavy-duty nutcracker.

Hibernaculum

There's no doubt they're there;
in the early morning you hear
the jiggery-pokery going on,
the give-away crusty-rustle
of hoglets snouting for slugs,
or scratching their flea-circus
into action under the leaf-heap
that's overgrown an old broom.
They're climbing all over her,
her secret, not what you think,
the one big thing she knows –
how to turn sharp into soft.

Dr Maimonides (i)
After *Treatise on Cohabitation*, c. 1190.

Physicians, apothecaries,
our art is long; cleave to the oath –
all that you hear shall not be spread abroad.

Consider the delicate case I present,
Sultan Al-Malik, Lord make his glory eternal,
the potentate is impotent; wasted in the seraglio,

as an Abyssinian eunuch or sliced cucumber.
His body withered to a lean sheaf;
too much heat, we will agree,

overexertion of the male organ
in a constitution predisposed to fire
– a familiar state, not difficult to treat

under a moderate regime if the patient is compliant.
But the Revered Master has impressed on us
the need for *increased* activity,

mindful of his maidens' number.
Additionally, according to his will,
I have selected only remedies

whose performance is pleasant
and easy to carry out. Am I,
Moses the Israelite from Cordova,

to give the Sultan lessons
in limits? Good fortune favoured
my research with a wondrous formula

that will enable the phallus
to remain tumescent,
even after the spilling of seed:

take 280 drachmas each of carrot oil,
radish oil, 70 drachmas mustard oil,
and combine with 140 drachmas of live

saffron-coloured ants. Set the oil in the sun
for at least a week before massaging
into the acorn of manhood for three hours

prior to intercourse; then wash in warm water.
Gentlemen, the affinity of testicle and radish,
carrot and male member, goes without saying;

the homology of mustard seed and human seed,
the power of the vital principle – orange –
in living ants, may be called into question

and if the patient prefers to eat a cake,
take: 22 drachmas of rooster bollocks,
with an equivalent amount of sparrow brain,

combine with 20 yolks of dove eggs,
adding cinnamon, mace, anise,
ground and sifted carnation,

before roasting in sesame oil.
But I can assure you the original medicament
uninscribed until now,

is efficacious,
and nothing comparable
has been found for this purpose.

Philosopher
i.m. P.F. Strawson

As I roll the wheels forward,
the sound of gears fast-spinning
the reel axis so that the five helices
describe a rotating steel cylinder
whose carefully adjusted height
is less than the width of a blade of grass
from the cutting bar on its sole plate,
reminds me of you in your garden,
most genteel of mowers,
dressed in a single-breasted suit
and panama, analysing the lawn,
methodically scything leaves,
as if they were logical errors grown
in Russell's 'Theory of Descriptions',
and you were 'The wise King of France'
in a poem that was neither true nor false.

Heritage

If I hadn't been there when Abraham
spotted a ram
and sheathed his knife,
my wrists wouldn't know
what it is to be freed.

If I hadn't been Judas,
had betrayed no one,
never pursed my lips,
my head wouldn't know
how to hang.

If I hadn't crossed the Pyrenees
on the back of an elephant
in Hannibal's army,
my hand wouldn't know
how to rise in a fist.

If I hadn't kissed the ground
in the court of Vizier al-Fadil,
broken bread at Maimonides' table,
I would never have read
the *Book of Poisons*.

If I hadn't sweated on Devil's Island,
and Zola hadn't been choked
on my behalf,
my heart wouldn't know
how to open in friendship.

If I hadn't lived
before I was born,
my eyes wouldn't know
how to weep
for my people.

The Medieval Jewish Cemetery In Oxford

Hot-houses rise
where the river bends at Magdalen Bridge,
watering birds of paradise.
A gentle society of plants
beyond the city wall—
no vestige of a headstone or a pall
to mark the buried souls.

In Piotrokow my fathers' graves
went under the plough,
they are not there.

Time and silence quiet the old Jews—
graceful stems of Kerria
stand in memoriam,
wearing their yellow stars
like the Danish King.

The medieval Jewish cemetery in Oxford, now a botanic garden, was escheated to the Crown in 1290 when the Jews were expelled from England.

There is a legend that the Danish King Christian X wore a yellow 'Star of David' during the Nazi occupation.

Buchenwald

Gustav Klimt, 1903, oil on canvas

up-stretched trees stand among the wasted leaves in memory of the future

Dr Maimonides (ii)
After *Treatise on Poisons*, c. 1198.

Your servant has examined the remedies
used by physicians for poisonous bites,
and found them to be generally warming.

Some are imbibed with wine,
others with water; if the patient is hot,
vinegar or milk should be used.

The scorpion's sting chills a person
to the core; in this case ampelos
is the preferred decoction.

For those to whom it is forbidden,
anise will do; like the ethrog seed
it counteracts any fatal toxin.

It is better to avoid being bitten
and if a man is chased by a snake,
he should flee into a sandy place.

A woman, on the other hand,
should make herself naked
and cohabit (with her husband)

in front of the animal. Some say
this will only inflame the serpent's
instinct. Rather she should

pull out a skein of hair,
gather a pile of nail parings
and hurl them at the attacker,

open her lips and shriek, 'I am unclean'.
If this fails to deter and the bite is fatal,
the serpent should be put to death

by a court of twenty-three.
But according to Rabbi Akiba,
it should be killed without a trial.

The Salon of Henriette Herz c. 1800
for Dr Peter Agulnik

Damen und Herren, It is a privilege to be able to introduce my dear friend, Professor Johann Christian Reil. We are most honoured that he can be with us tonight. He has travelled especially from Halle where he was Professor Extraordinarius and is now Professor Ordinarius and Director of the Clinical Institute. His ideas are far from ordinary. Johann believes that we are made out of stuff. And that the human mind is a mere epiphenomenon, deriving from the chemical and anatomical structure of the body. The care of the insane should therefore rightly be in the hands of physicians. They need to be trained in the treatment of the soul, for which he has coined a new term – *psychiatry*. Mental illness can be cured. But once having discharged a patient from the madhouse, who will cure that "greater fools' house" that is the rest of the world? Within the innocuous confines of the asylum, he remarks, "no villages smoke and no people moan in their own blood". Despite the mind's material origin, the higher functions are susceptible to psychological influence.

Patients inclined to remain in a state of continuous reverie can be rescued from their irrational dreams and returned to a state of full consciousness by being forced to listen to a fugue played on the *katzenpiano*. As an illustration of his system of care, what he calls "non-injurious torture", Johann will be giving us a demonstration on this remarkable instrument. I crave your indulgence whilst he voices the apparatus with a suitable number of cats. You will notice that it looks much like a normal *upright* except that the animals are arranged in a row inside the body of the piano, with tails stretched out behind them and heads locked in a series of holes jigged out of the wooden top. A keyboard fitted out with sharpened nails will be set over the cats so that they can be struck in order to provide the sound. Professor Reil assures me that a piece of music rendered – when the ill person is so placed that he cannot miss the expressions on their faces and the play of these creatures – must even now bring Lot's wife out of her salt block.

See LeeAnn Hansen, ' Metaphors of Mind and Society: The Origins of German Psychiatry in the Revolutionary Era', *Isis*, 89, (1998), 387-409 and Robert Richards, 'Rhapsodies on a Cat-Piano, or Johann Christian Reil and the Foundations of Romantic Psychiatry', *Critical Inquiry*, 24, (1998), pp. 700-702.

Musée Rodin

As she demonstrates how Adam and Eve
in *The Hand of God*, can be spun
on a turn-table for the digital camera,
the museum guide tells us *The Gates of Hell*
is an allegory. *The Three Shadows* are closing
their fists over the impossibilities of Hellenism –
Paulo's stolen *Kiss*, chaste as a perfect curve,
his palm marbling Francesca's thigh,
as if it were *The Thinker's* chin. His touch,
sexy as a horsefly on a mare's haunch;
the glassy-eyed amble of the crowd
through Rilke's office in the Hôtel Biron,
like window-shoppers at Le Bon Marché –
abandon hope who enter here, no raunch ,
no lust, just the money-spinning knick-knacks
on display, minted according to a classic formula.

Spoilage

Who would sever the earth's aorta?
There's black blood between us,
pulsed out of the depth.

Crude coagulates its riches,
tars the seabirds
to a lumpen species.
Dark horses gallop
the ocean.

The mind unfathoms.

Nothing can tamp what's lost,
dregs smack their gobshite
against the foulmouthed shore,
agog with gargle.

When the tide's drained,
no ark
will ground on Ararat.

Koro

Koro: anxiety and fear that the penis will retract into the abdomen and cause death. ICD-10 Classification of Mental and Behavioural Disorders F48.8

My *Speedo* goggles cling like nursing babes, misty as lovers' eyes; fixed on a
thin black line I slide up and down like an abacus bead, counting
one one one one, two two two two. A young Australian
is measuring his lengths in multiples of K.
Nobody in the locker-room minds
the floor, powdered like a pastry-board,
smeared with a damp mop; generations
of athletes have trodden here,
you would think it safe
as a shop-window
to sneak a look
at yourself drying
off see the expansion
of your pectorals,
but for the old man
in the mirror with
his ballooning
hydrocele, penis
invaginated into
scrotum like
a retreating
tortoise, or
toad-in-the
-hole. I
doubt I'm
well enough
to be saved
by emergency
fellatio.
Unwinding
after exercise
people are
prone to
whistle
and sing—
God only
knows what
about
?

Flood

Water came in from the west,
   dashed in horizontal surges,
     urgently butting the door,
        pounding the roof's corrugations
          with its drenched fists like a lynch mob,
            like a dawn raid, spilling over rain gutters,
              downpipes, flushing rock and mud
                off the hills, filling flumes, sink-holes,
                  channels, tributaries, streaming gullies,
                    furrows, bringing sheep
skulls, dead birds,
                        torn tree
   limbs, wool floccules,
                        horse
   manure, rusted iron fence poles,
                        blue
plastic slivers, grass clods,
                        delaminated soles,
gush and spume,
                  a fluxion through the
village,
              like a ruddled, dog-driven flock,
           a tide, a flowage, an open sluice
         splashing over blocked drains,
        the irresistible rush washing through,
          as if God had uncreated a firmament,
            unleashed a sea against the gable
ends,
                  an ingress like a
        liberating army
                    or long-lost
      mother, reclaiming
                      stones
                    quarried from
the river,

       as if our dry houses

       had never been their homes.

Trap Grounds

In May 2006, six acres of wetland, scrubland, and woodland in north-west Oxford were saved from development after a House of Lords ruling confirmed that the scrubland could be registered as a Town Green. No one knows how the place acquired its name.

Birds may have been caught here,
or eels trapped in baskets
made of willow withies.

Pony traps could have been left
in the area during Sheriff's Races,
or it might have been a site

where night-soil was dumped,
the word being slang for 'privy'.
Some say 'trap' stood for 'extra parochial',

denoting the fact that this land
was exempt from tithes.
Sounds make their escape –

the muntjac's pack of dogs,
yaffle of a green woodpecker,
the water rail's piggish squeal.

Lampyris Noctiluca

Glow worm, you're a sexy beast,
except you haven't got a mouth
or wings, and aren't a worm.

There's only one thing you live for –
every segment
of your being,

waiting, every second of your time,
each night
at sundown,

hoping desperately,
giving out the green light
to any cruising male.

You'll have a mouth
in your next life,
something to die for.

Turdus Merula

J'avais l'oiseau dans ma cage –
bird in my basket of willow,
your black throat quavers
a restive song.

Mais l'oiseau s'est envolé –
ebony arrow out of the quiver,
your long streak
away from me.

Perspective

Mountains, blue-grey
always in the distance—
the colour of memory,
of eucalyptus,
pipe-smoke curling,
washed-out jeans,
departing trains.
Blue-grey, the colour
of impossibility.
You, in the foreground,
moving on to pastures green.

Canzone
after Petrarch No: 74

I'm sick and tired
of my obsession with you –
I go on and on;
whatever I do I'm stuck

talking in my sleep
about your eyes, your hair,
on a hiding to nowhere. No one
can get my one track mind

to alter course. I'm like
some pathetic stalker
wasting the time of my life

on poems like this.
Whose fault's that?
Love, I suppose, not art.

Aegithalos Caudatus

They keep on knocking at the window,
one of these days those long-tailed tits
are going to burst right in, like burglars
or police or stuntmen smashing through
glass or ice-breakers or successful sperm
or cricket balls hurled at greenhouses
or psychopathic postmen or slung stones
or members of The Bullingdon Club
or sharpshooters' bullets or big-bad-wolves
or men whose wives wind them up
or children playing blind man's buff
or blind drunk men or ham-fisted glaziers
or karate black belts or kamikaze pilots
or poison arrows or cupid's darts
or overzealous narcissists in a hall of mirrors
or dolphins breaking the sea's surface
or mad lovers after a long separation
or torpedoes or armour-piercing shells
or high-flying businesswomen. It's not
as if they're getting anything out of it.
Just because of the size of their tail,
who the hell do those fluffed-up headbangers
                              think they are?

Laundry Basket

Imagine the creel full of trout,
silver for the table, hitched on
a shoulder and carried home.

My catch was underwear,
socks that got away, posted in
the slot on top back to the wash.

A romance with bric-a-brac,
but were they in it from the start—
sleepers cradled in wicker cribs,

weapons buried in secret silos?
Just how long had that fishy skep
been cribbled by grubs, dusting

osier over all the dirty clothes—
a beetle-flight that meant
to bring the whole house down.

Property of Tesco

Lying on its top in a ditch,
an underfunded landing craft
or alien hunted down and
left for dead, legs upward
in robotic rigor mortis,
as if waiting for a miracle
of aerodynamics that would
spin life into the wheels
or trying to transmit a signal—
No doubt beyond our galaxy
there's a Mission Control,
banks of rocket scientists
watching screens, clicking mice,
quietly going off their trolley.

Hirundo Rustica

Beyond the horizon of my poem,
swooped the room at head height,
winging the kitchen then back;
some demented dumbellina,
window-thumper, ceiling-basher,
panic-monger.

All of a sudden quiet, out of sight,
perhaps behind a chair.
And then it starts,
the fear transfers, we're wasps confined
in a beer mug, or bats who've lost their sonar.
Laptop's a bird trap.

How can I write a word, when any time
I open my mind, it might fly in?

Lady Walk
(Hawthornden Castle)

A fan of crow
flamencos open,
foxed into afterlife;
who would believe a doe
could eye you
for more than a split
second,
rustle the invisible
lòke a hare?
Even a tiny spider
can tread on air.

Frondeg

If Major Kovalyov's nose could leave his face
and lead a life of its own; if Bottom could wake up
to find himself an ass, Gregor Samsa become an insect,
why not Prof. David Alan Kepesh a mammary gland?

Weird in Roth's New York, but here the mind's
suckled on mutations – after moving in
we learned the etymology of the name,
morphed out of 'bron' and 'teg' –

we were living inside a *Beautiful Breast*;
or maybe two knocked together, the narrow steps
that once spiralled over the hearth at either end,
now blocked and replaced by a central stairway,

a cleavage between the two sides of the house.
Over time, the walls of the building began to sag,
the areolated limestone weathered to an ancient dresser,
where migrant swallows hung their earthen cups.

Winter in *Frondeg*

How can I sketch this night?
Pages wrapped in silence,
you drawing my head in a beanie.
The breath of burning wood,
the pressure of your foot swaddled
in three socks shifting on the table,
and the small intervals between
pencil-strokes that are quiet
as thoughts, lighter than snow.

Alexandrian Duet

Antony:
They say what's in my head is a waste of space,
I'd have it out now, if I could,
And fill the cavity with something worth while –
Your bed-linen, for example, or the screwed-up
Papyrus you were writing on yesterday,
Could it have been a love-poem?
As it is, I'll have to wait. They can put a hook
Up my nose after I'm dead, cribble my brain,
Yank the whole lot out to feed the jackals,
It'd be a relief. This may be too much to ask,
But I'd like it to be your fragrant hands
That reach in to harvest my liver and lungs,
Jar up my guts, lave the inner surface
Of my abdomen with oil, freshly pressed
from the fruit of that red palm, whose leaves
I've often noticed, just outside the window
Above your bed. I don't trust the sons of Horus.
If there's sod all in one's head, what difference
Human, baboon or falcon? Being disembowelled,
Even for a short period, isn't something to relish …

But if it's necessary for the sake of future fitness,
I'll go along with it; don't over-stuff me though,
So that I look obese. I don't want to look or smell
Like that putrefying heap of garbage, Wakhakwi,
I've caught him giving you the eye on more
Than one occasion. That's a joke we should keep
To ourselves. I'd rather be drained on a board,
Cleansed with natron like a well-scrubbed table.
And for the record, you'll be in my giant scarab
Of a heart, scented with myrrh and cinnamon,
Which I hope you don't forget to put back inside,
For every one of those forty days and nights.
Death's not anything really, well only a nuisance
Your way, because it's such a to-do, all that
Wrapping and gluing. I don't need protection,
Especially by some hairless priests. There's nothing
more powerful than our love. Let's say
I'm confident soul and body will be reunited,

Just as we shall always be together, my cock's
Jutting like a god's at the mere thought of it.
Cleopatra:
Ah! beloved griffin, forget the organ in your head
That's only good for oozing rheum –
Do you recall, general, how I cast my spell at Tarsus,
Hexed you, when you thought to conquer me,
Right under Ra's golden nose? They say his bones
Shook with laughter, dripped melted silver on my oars,
When he saw me clip your wings. Had you been Wakhakwi,
I wouldn't have risked the Cydnus under purple sail,
Reclined like Aphrodite, fanned by beautiful boys.
Would I have dressed my maidens as Sea-nymphs,
Had them work the galley to the sound of flute and harp,
Perfumed the vessel with Metopion? At sunset,
When a bouquet of cardamom hung in the air,
Supped you under a panoply of lights, hidden in tall trees
Like a flock of cockatoos? We banqueted on heron,
Roasted wild swan, spiced with cumin and coriander,
Onion globes like giants' testicles, to stimulate the appetite;
Pomegranate, water melon, dates and grapes and figs.
In our cups, I took your ear by surprise with ribald jokes,
Oh yes! The Queen of Egypt understood Marc Antony.

What say we roll the dice tonight, and if you lose,
I'll almond-shape your eyes with Mesdemet,
Wear a mask myself and dress in rags?
We'll bare our chests and carry castanets,
No one will know it's us. They'll think we're
Drunken low-lives on the razzle or dancers
From a pageant having fun. You have to mime
A hippopotamus, I'll ride you down the Nile,
Carouse the town. Then you can smack your lips,
Unhinge jaws, creep slowly in the sand
Like a hungry crocodile, and I'll play scared.
No doubt you'll pick a quarrel in the street,
You always do, as if it's in your blood,
Like fighting fowl or bulls that lock horns,
Or maybe it's just Romans, what do you think?
Don't get me wrong, I'm fond of men who brawl;
It's like erotic art, it turns me on. And afterward

We'll rollick home, I'll clean your wounds,
Massage aching muscles with henna oil,
Share a bath with you in ass's milk.

These Forms

                      I can't throw out,
have the unmeasure of you,
a kind of negative c.v.
I painstakingly scribed –
the life of the maggot in your mind

that hated soap; its appetite
for leather wormed into your shoe's
unrepaired sole. The griffin claw
of your big toe-nail it wouldn't trim;
the help it stopped from coming in.

It conned you into getting on
a one one three without your fare
and then forgetting where you were
or why you were there;
it never cared –

the summer dress you wore
in mid-winter, with its pattern
of strawberry stains; it made you
embrace strangers as best friends,
forget your children's names;

but some enchanted evening, couldn't damp
the scent of lilacs gathered in the spring
or crack the pleasure dome in Xanadu,
that was the you
                    they never asked about.

Lifting Anchor

On such a morning I'd rise with the sun,
swim to shore and loose the stern line
from its tree trunk, as you fastened hatches
and gathered in the slack,
then watch the plough-flukes come up,
glinting like fish-silver.

On such a morning the barometer read high,
we'd breakfast on yoghurt and honey,
examine the horizon for a caravan of tents,
pitched in the haze. We'd cleat off the halliard
and set course to the wind,
where the sea prepared a festival of scrolls.

On such a morning we'd winch
the mainsail tight, sheet in the genoa
till the tell-tales settled their nerves,
and we could taste weather
over the starboard gunwale,
and the day was seasoned with hope.

Last Will

Yes, a cardboard box will do,
it suits my style. And plant
a broad-leafed tree over my grave;
let its roots dig down deep,
soak me up while lovers fuck
beneath its rustling canopy
on a bed of maidenhair.
Save me from a rococo end,
a brass casket, a carved stone,
a rose-garden on a floribunda theme.
I want to decompose
where others writhe and moan.

The Art of Disappearing

It takes a lifetime to hone,
but no one fails to get there in the end.
Study the occultation of lights,
the properties of mist, the iridescence
on the surface of a soap-bubble.
Investigate the guttering of candles
and the screw of the vortex,
the history of Stalin's airbrush.
Pay close attention to the behaviour of birds;
their games of grandmother's footsteps,
skill in evacuation at short notice,
the unseen flight of a sparrow hawk;
or learn a lesson from the wild duck,
no magic, nothing tucked under the wing –
watch the crook in the fowler's finger,

now you see me

Made in the USA
Charleston, SC
15 April 2013